Happiness
is Just a
Thought Away

Written by David Gibson

Illustrated by Michael Warren

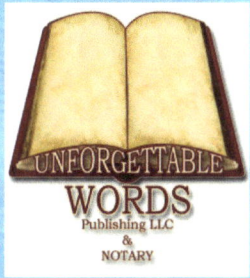

Happiness is Just a Thought Away

©2010 **David Gibson**

No toxic materials were used in the manufacturing of this book.

All rights reserved. No part of this publication may be reproduced, stored in any retrieval system, or transmitted in any form or by any means, mechanical, photocopying, recording, or otherwise, without permission in writing from the publisher, except by a reviewer, who may quote brief passages in a review.

Manufactured in the United States of America

For information please contact:

Unforgettable Words Publishing LLC
Summerville SC 29485
www.unforgettablewords.club

"The Power of words"

ISBN-13: 978-0-9969445-0-2

ISBN-10: 0-9969445-0-8

LCCN: 2010912834

Contact Information

unforgettablewords.club@gmail.com

www.unforgettablewords.club

This book is dedicated to everyone who has ever had hardships or a bad day.

I would like to thank God for this book's simple yet poignant message that is not just for children, but for young and old hearts.

I want to thank my family for being my inspiration, especially my kids, who keep reminding me that happiness is just a thought away.

Thanks to those who took the time to read this to their children or to themselves.

Thanks to all who stood behind me through this process and believe in the message of this book.

What's the difference between being **bored** and being **relaxed**?

How can you have a good time preparing a meal and creating a **huge mess**?

By getting family and friends to decide which dish they like the **best**.

www.ingramcontent.com/pod-product-compliance
Lightning Source LLC
Chambersburg PA
CBHW041126300426

44113CB00002B/82